On An Average Day

John Kolvenbach's other plays include *The Gravity of Means,*
On the Fritz, and *Gizmo Love*

Published by Methuen 2003

1 3 5 7 9 10 8 6 4 2

First published in 2003 by
Methuen Publishing Limited
215 Vauxhall Bridge Road
London SW1V 1EJ

Methuen Publishing Limited Reg. No. 3543167

A CIP catalogue record for this book is available from the British Library

ISBN 0 413 77328 0

Typeset by SX Composing DTP, Rayleigh, Essex
Printed and bound in Great Britain by
Cox & Wyman Ltd, Reading, Berkshire

On An Average Day

by

John Kolvenbach

Methuen Drama

For Roanne and the Baker

On An Average Day was first produced in London by Sonia Friedman, Dede Harris, Mort Swinsky and Act Productions, performed at the Comedy Theatre, London on 25 July 2002. The cast was as follows:

Robert   Woody Harrelson
Jack   Kyle MacLachlan

Directed by John Crowley
Designed by Scott Pask
Lighting by Mark Henderson
Sound design Aura

The play was produced with Best Case Scenario LLC by arrangement with Charlotte Road Productions.

Characters

Robert, forty
Jack, forty-seven

Jack and Robert may be younger. Robert may be as young as thirty. What is fixed, though, is the difference in their ages, seven years.

Act One

A kitchen. A grimy relic, unchanged in thirty years.

A man sits at a table. He drinks purposefully from a sixteen-ounce can of beer. A bottle of bourbon waits, uncapped. The man, forty, is gaunt and somewhat sallow. He wears soiled clothes. He drinks.

Another man enters without knocking. He is older, forty-seven. He is weary, resigned. He holds a brown paper lunch bag. The object inside the bag gives it heft.

Between the men, a resemblance. The younger man stands. He speaks.

Robert Jack.

Pause. Neither moves.

I didn't do it, Jack.

*Pause. Then **Jack** places the lunch bag on the counter.*

Want a beer or something. (What'd you, make me a sandwich?)

*Pause. **Jack** doesn't respond.*

Jack? I got a beer in the fridge if you want one.

*A pause, in which **Jack**'s continued stillness disturbs **Robert**.*

(*An offering.*) The shower started working again.

Pause.

Is this a mute thing now that's developed? You wanna piece of chalk?

Jack How're you doing, Bob?

Robert I'm OK, I can taste this metal thing trying to crawl out of my throat every once in a while but it doesn't make it all the way out, ever, so I'm OK, I've been all right.

Jack (*without sarcasm*) That's good to hear.

Robert   I didn't do it, Jack.

Jack   You said that.

Pause, and still, **Jack** *stands just inside the doorway.*

Robert   You want a beer or something? You want, like, a beer or something?

Jack   All right.

Robert (*not approaching* **Jack**, *pointing warily to the refrigerator*) I got probably, I dunno, any number of beers in there, whatever you wanna do.

Jack *crosses to the refrigerator. He opens it. An awful smell.*

Jack   Good *Christ*.

He slams the refrigerator closed, recoiling.

Robert (*unsurprised*)   Yeah.

Jack (*breathing into his hand, repulsed*)   *Jesus.*

Robert   You gotta try to be quick with it.

Jack (*re: the smell*)   What *is* that?

Robert   I shoulda said something, it's best to be pretty quick with that thing.

Jack   What's *in* there?

Robert   I usually get two out. If I'm gonna get one I go ahead and get two most of the time, saves you half the thing.

Jack   It *smells*.

Robert   It doesn't seem to get on the can.

Jack   It's un*natural*.

Robert   You'd think it'd adhere to the top of the can? But I've pretty much checked into it, it doesn't, so I wouldn't worry about it.

Jack   It *stinks*.

Robert (*irritably*)   What do you want me to say.

Jack   Have you *looked* in there?

Robert   Well, yeah, Jack, the thing has a *light*.

Jack   Do you know what's *causing* it?

Robert (*suddenly volcanic*)   WHAT DO YOU WANT. DO YOU WANT A *GLASS*? WHAT. IT DOESN'T GET ON THE CAN! ALL RIGHT, JACK? I HAVE LOOKED INTO IT!

Pause. Then **Robert** *sits.*

Jack   You all right?

Robert   Yeah, I dunno, I got the thing of every time I go around a corner I think someone's gonna *scratch* me, all the time.

Jack (*sympathetically*)   Mmm.

Robert   It's disorientating.

Jack   Would be.

Robert   And I'm afraid I might fall down and just end *up* there, lying on the road or something.

Jack   Are you eating?

Robert (*surprised at the irrelevancy*)   Am I *what*?

Jack   Are you eating anything?

Robert   Am I eating?

Jack   Are you eating at all?

Robert   What does that have to do with anything?

Jack   Are you hungry?

Robert   Now?

Jack   You might try to eat.

Robert　As like, what, as maybe that would *change* something?

Jack (*alluding to entire kitchen*)　You have any food in here anywhere?

Robert　Why?

Jack　There any eggs?

Robert　For what?

Jack (*indicating the refrigerator*)　Is there any food in that thing?

Robert (*beat – surprised by the possibility*)　You wanna *cook* me something?

Jack　Do you have anything?

Robert (*touched*)　You're gonna fix me, like, an Omelette, Jack? You wanna cook me a Meal?

Jack　When did you eat last, d'you remember?

Robert (*then, openly, like a child*)　You think you might stay for a while, Jackie? (*Beat.*) Couple of weeks or anything? Stay around for a little while?

A pause in which **Jack** *doesn't answer.*

Jack　Bob –

Robert (*a kind of enticement*)　The shower started working, comes on outta nowhere all of a sudden. I'm always of the thing of you gotta take advantage whenever it comes around.

Jack (*re: whether he might stay a while*)　No, Bobby.

Robert (*re: the shower*)　It's like that comet.

Jack　Bob.

Robert　What's that bastard called? Every six million years?

Jack (*clearly*)   I'm not gonna stay a while.

Pause. **Robert** *will attempt to hide his disappointment.*

Jack   I don't want you thinking something.

Robert   No, I know.

Jack   I'm not gonna be around.

Robert   I know, I'm just saying.

Jack   I know you are.

Robert   I'm just like, asking the thing out loud, air the thing out a little.

Jack   All right.

Robert   It's informational.

Jack   OK.

Pause.

Robert (*re: his general well-being, lying*)   I'm all *right*.

Jack (*lying*)   You seem it.

Robert (*with false courage*)   Things change, Jack.

Jack   Sure.

Robert   Either that or they don't and just because you wake up a certain way on Monday doesn't mean anything's gonna feel like that tomorrow: you get what you pay for, fuck it.

Pause. He found no comfort in his aphorism.

What's that saying?

Jack   I don't know.

Robert (*tries again, bravely*)   Don't expect the hopeful scenario is gonna happen based on your expectations or anything 'cause you'll get screwed by how most stuff is different.

Jack (*re: the length of his stay*) I'm sorry, Bob.

Robert No, come on, that's not even how the saying goes anyway, my whole brain is half scrambled, the actual saying is like, I don't even *know* what, Happy.

Jack How about a beer, Bob, you want one?

Pause. **Robert** *doesn't respond.*

Robert (Regular person, you ask him if he wants a beer, he doesn't have to check first if it might make him throw up.)

Pause. **Jack** *appraises* **Robert**.

(Also most guys aren't thinking in terms of: a beer might end up feeding the metal thing in my throat, causing it to grow and choke me to death. Most guys, that's not a consideration.)

Jack (*with concern*) (Bobby.)

Robert Fuck it though actually, seriously.

Jack (You all right?)

Robert (I'm a little up and down.)

Jack (You seem it.)

Robert (What comes out, I'm surprised *myself* at some of it, don't pay attention.)

Pause.

Jack (How about I get you that beer, Bobby?)

Robert (OK.)

Jack (All right?)

Robert (Yeah.)

Jack (*then, crossing to the refrigerator*) See if I can brave the Mad Smell you got tied up in here.

Robert (*emerging*) You sure you're up to it?

Jack   Built up a little Immunity from the last time, I'm hoping.

Robert   Maybe don't be so ultra-Sensitive, give *that* a shot.

Jack (*to* **Robert**, *standing at the refrigerator*)   You ready?

Robert   (Will you look at the olfactory Courage from this guy all of a sudden?)

Jack   (Seriously, Bob, you should consider cleaning the thing out some time.)

Robert   (Out of *no*where, he's the man of nasal *steel*.)

Jack (*his hand on the handle*)   Are you *ready*?

Robert   Be quick with it, Jack, I'm not kidding.

Jack   I'm gonna try.

Robert   Takes a certain amount of Aggression.

Jack *opens the refrigerator. An awful smell. He snatches four beers grouped in a plastic six-pack ring. He slams the door, puts his hand to his face.*

Jack   *Damn*.

Robert (*beat – surprised, pleased, encouraged*)   You got four!

Jack   I just grabbed in there.

Robert   Two each, Jack, you did it *perfectly*.

Jack   I got lucky.

Robert (*ebulliently*)   You got a familiarity with the appliance, is what you *got*.

Jack   That's probably true.

Robert   Probably my ass, Jack, you got a home-field *advantage*.

Jack (*re: the smell*)   (Jesus, does burn the eyes a little.)

Robert   *Toss* me one of those things, throw one of those bastards over here. (You got *Citizenship*, Jack, good for a *Life*time.)

Jack (*tossing a beer to* **Robert**, *then inspecting his own*)   (You said there's not anything *on* here?)

Robert   You wanna know something?

Jack   (I wonder if you can't smell it on the lid 'cause your nose has just been scalded.)

Robert   Jack?

Jack   Yeah.

Robert   You wanna know something?

Jack   What's that.

Robert (*positively*)   And I don't even know if I'm gonna be able to get enough emphasis on the thing to actually convey the whole size of it, but us in the kitchen at the same time together? Here's me and apparently there are you? I can't even start to say how *strange* that is.

Jack   Well, cheers Bob.

Robert   'Cause I already told you about the metal thing and the who's gonna scratch me around every corner thing. Knowing these things are outside the Norm, makes me question like: are you actually even *standing* there.

Jack   I'm right here.

Robert   Which is borderline Miraculous, Jack, the thing is *Religious* either way, is what I'm trying to make *Clear*, is that either I'm somebody who's having *Visions*, or it's the other thing, which is: Here you Are.

Jack   Yeah. (*Beat.*) Well, it's been a while, I guess.

Pause.

Robert   Listen, I know what you're gonna say.

Jack   Bobby, stop it, all right?

Robert   I'm curious.

Jack   Will you stop?

Robert   But it's on my whole *mind*, Jack, I can't open my mouth, or it automatically comes *out*.

Jack   So stop talking, how about.

Robert   No, but is this one of those things where you're gonna be around for like a *month*?

Jack   Bob.

Robert   Is that a possibility?

Jack   I said this.

Robert   Is a month, like, in the *vicinity*?

Jack   No. It's not in the vicinity.

Robert (*encouraged by* **Jack***'s specificity*)   So this is what I'm asking. Is it a *six*-month kind of thing?

Jack   I'm here now.

Robert   So it's like a day-to-day thing, it's like a who-knows thing.

Jack   I'm not staying.

Robert   But at least through the trial, though, right? to the end at least.

Jack   The trial.

Robert   Which, the length is sort of up in the air, so you'd be in one of those day-to-day deals.

Jack   The trial.

Robert   (It's not all Grim and Drag, Jack.)

Jack   (What?)

Robert   (There's some upside in there.)

Jack   (What are we talking about?)

Robert   (You know how if you get put in contact with individuals you might not *know*, normally, how there's some Information there?)

Jack   (OK.)

Robert   (This is one of those.)

Jack   (What is?)

Robert   (Only I gotta say, the only information I have so far is: Who the fuck *are* these people?)

Jack   (Who?)

Robert (*an outburst*)   The *One* Guy, God, the FAT SCHMUCK.

Jack   Whoa, Bobby.

Robert   You should *see* this guy!

Jack   From the trial?

Robert   My *motive*, like he's got access to my *mind* all of a sudden.

Jack   A lawyer.

Robert   A *douche*bag.

Jack   A lawyer, this is.

Robert   What's the *matter* with that guy?

Jack   I don't know –

Robert   The People *Versus*, like suddenly he's a *plural*, he's the royal *We*. (Fucking queen.)

Jack   A prosecutor.

Robert   ('Member that time in Scouts, Jack? and Jimmy Rapanti borrowed my hatchet or something and then he kept saying it was his and so you and me went over to his house and kicked his ass?)

Jack (*warily*)   . . . Why?

Robert   Remember that?

Jack   Maybe.

Robert   I think about that sometimes.

Jack   In what context.

Robert   In like, what if the Fat Schmuck is in the phone book?

Jack   The lawyer?

Robert   What if the fat load is *listed*?

Jack   Bob.

Robert   How about in the context of you and me pulling into his driveway with the lights off. How about you and me in *that* context?

Jack (*quite firmly*)   Bob? That is a Very Bad idea.

Robert   Remember that Jimmy Rapanti thing?

Jack   It's a Bad idea, Bobby.

Robert   That whole year. You remember that? People were half afraid to even *talk* to me that year.

Jack   That's a *positive*.

Robert   Who talks to the Lone Ranger?

Jack   What?

Robert   *Nobody*.

Jack   What about Tonto?

Robert   That's what I'm saying, so maybe you and I weren't exactly *popular*.

Jack   You were *seven*.

Robert   I was *right*, was what I was.

Jack You were *what?*

Robert Jimmy's *face*, and I don't wanna sound like I *enjoyed* something –

Jack You were *right?*

Robert Jimmy understood that we came from a thing of *Fury* –

Jack (*suddenly, fiercely*) IT WASN'T YOUR HATCHET.

Pause.

Robert It didn't turn *out* to be my hatchet.

Jack What does that even *mean?*

Robert We *thought* it was, Jack.

Jack *So?*

Robert So at the *time*, I'm saying, that was a justified thing at that *time*, given our thinking at that particular –

Jack Bob. We Are Not Going to Anybody's House. We are Not Pulling into Anybody's *Driveway* with the Lights Off, all *right?*

Pause.

Jack *Bob.*

Robert All *right.*

Jack I'm serious.

Robert I'm not saying let's go get in the *car*, Jack, Jesus, I'm just thinking about how here you are and suddenly that's a *possibility*.

Jack It's *not* a possibility.

Robert *OK.*

Jack And even if it *Was*, Bob, if it was an *Option*, it would be a *Stupid* option, OK? and *not* Justified and not anything there's even a *Chance* of us doing.

Robert   Jesus, I'm *talking*, guy can *talk*. Options happen to be *optional*, Jack, that's most of their whole *make*up. We may not necessarily *choose* to, but isn't it great to know we *can* –

Jack   IT WASN'T YOUR *HATCHET*.

Pause.

Robert (*cowed*)   Christ, Jack, all *right*, I was a little *kid*, it's not even what I'm *talking* about.

Jack (*exasperated, massaging his upper nose*)   (Jesus Christ.)

Robert   I'm saying good to see you, is my whole point: good to see you around the kitchen again, is all I'm saying.

Jack   Oh, *that's* what you're saying.

Robert   Yeah and How're you doing, that kind of thing.

Jack   (I forgot what you were like.)

Robert   You have a headache?

Jack (*not asking*)   (How long have I been here.)

Robert (*offering the bourbon*)   You wanna give this guy a little action?

Jack (*asking*)   How long have I been here?

Robert   Take a smidgen outta this dog here, Jack, good for you.

Jack *accepts the bottle. He drinks.*

Jack (*re: something unknown*)   (. . . Goddammit.)

Pause.

Robert (*a kind of peace offering*)   You wanna hop in the shower, get off some of that road grime or anything . . . thing's working again, like I told you . . .

Pause.

(*Another attempt to begin a peaceful exchange.*) Out of the blue, thing gets very enthusiastic all of a sudden.

Jack (*softening, engaging*)   You two have that in common.

Robert   The shower and me.

Jack   Very enthusiastic all of a sudden.

Robert   Me and the shower.

Jack   Yeah.

Robert   You might wanna add your*self* to that list you got there, Jack.

Jack (*with a little laugh*)   . . . I'll do that.

Robert   Know what I'm saying?

Jack (*opening his second beer*)   Guess it must run in the family.

Robert (*re:* **Jack***'s beer*)   (See? now you got two out, you don't have to get another one out this time.)

Jack   (It's a great system, Bob.)

Pause.

Robert (*making conversation*)   I'm telling you, Jack, out of *no*where, this thing. Thing starts acting like a shower again.

Jack   Fascinating.

Robert   It actually messed up some stuff I had stored in the tub in there, got a whole bunch of belongings I had all soaked and pretty much ruined.

Jack   You had some stuff in the shower?

Robert   Some newspapers got all ruined.

Jack   You had newspapers in the *shower*?

Robert   I had a collection.

Jack   Of *newspapers*?

Robert   Anytime there was an anonymous body found somewhere, somebody they couldn't figure out who it was, I would save the paper.

Jack (*beat*)   *Why?*

Robert   So if, you know, if a whole bunch of people were burned beyond recognition, anything with an unidentified dead person, I would save that day's edition, just in case.

Jack   In case *what?*

Robert   I expanded it to like, crank callers and any kind of kidnapper type, anybody Unidentified, I would save all of those papers, and obviously that's almost every day's thing, took up a lot of room. So why not stick 'em in the shower eventually (thing hasn't worked in a decade), and it got to be a big pile.

Jack   Just in case *what*, Bobby?

Pause.

Bob?

Robert (*beat. A confession*)   . . . In case one of the unidentified people turns out to be someone I know.

Jack   Like who?

Robert   . . . Or in case one turns out to be me.

Pause.

Jack (*sympathetically, and as if for the first time*)   How've you been, Bobby?

Pause.

Robert (*considering*)   How am I?

Jack   Are you all right?

Robert   . . . Yeah . . .

Jack (*gently*)   You're all right?

Robert   No, you know, it can get pretty loud, Everybody hating you, it gets pretty loud some nights.

Pause.

Jack Are you married or anything?

Robert *What?*

Jack I dunno.

Robert Am I *married?*

Jack Yeah.

Robert To *who?*

Jack I don't know.

Robert I'm not *married,* Jack.

Jack OK.

Robert Why'd you say that?

Jack I thought it was a Possibility.

Robert Like what, you mean like Theoretically?

Jack I'm just asking, you seem a little disturbed.

Robert I'm fine.

Jack Well, that's clearly not the case.

Robert It what?

Jack You're not fine, Bob.

Robert Does that show?

Jack Does it *show?*

Robert I don't seem good?

Jack No.

Robert You *know* me though, there might be a thing of you seeing into some deeper layers of discomfort there.

Jack Objectively, Bob. You're a little unwell.

Robert These people *hate* me.

Jack From the trial.

Robert   You ever have a stranger hate your guts, Jack?

Jack   (. . . Christ, yeah, actually.)

Robert   It's un*settling*.

Jack   Why do they hate you?

Robert   *Why*? You should *hear* this Fat Schmuck.

Jack   The lawyer.

Robert (*again: suddenly, fully*)   *Jesus*, Jack, who *are* these people? *Honestly*.

Jack   He's unpleasant.

Robert   That's the *least* of his problems.

Jack   He's not reasonable.

Robert   He's not *palatable*.

Jack   He *is* a lawyer, Bob.

Robert (*an example*)   He's saying something. (You know these guys?) He's calling me *names*, probably. And the guy (every *time*, Jack) after he says the thing: he takes this little *pause*, after.

Jack   After the accusation.

Robert   He takes a *pause*! Right after whatever *horse*shit (you wouldn't *believe* the guy) this little *moment* to, like, recognize.

Jack   He takes a pause?

Robert   To *idolize* himself.

Jack   You serious?

Robert   You know these guys?

Jack   He does that?

Robert   Like, 'Did I just *say* that?' Some *sewage*, and then this *pause*, to go like –

Jack   To admire what he just said.

Robert   Where do these people *come* from?

Jack   I hate that.

Robert   Right?

Jack   Like what's the pause for, we should *clap*?

Robert   We should blow the guy?

Jack   Hate that.

Robert (*encouraged by* **Jack***'s response*)   Jack, the guy wears his *suit* like the thing is *patting* him on the *back*. Like his *tie* is *honored* to be wrapped around his fat *neck*.

Jack   He's *like* that?

Robert   Like his *shirt* is just *blushing* with Admiration, the *privilege*, to be tucked into the guy's *pants*. All its *life*, the shirt, if only it could spend a day pressed up against this guy's *ass*, this guy.

Jack   This is the shirt's thought process.

Robert   And it's not only the *shirt*.

Jack   The guy's admired.

Robert   The whole friggin' *country*.

Jack   They have the same thought.

Robert   They all think the same *way*! The *Judge* is like: How can I *lick* the Fat Schmuck?

Jack   Looking for a way to lick him in the recess.

Robert   The Jury of My Peers! (And lemme just say one thing for a second here: Where do they *find* these people? In my *life*, Jack, I have not *witnessed* such a collection of Freaks and Morons and Postal Clerks. You should *see* these people, it's like if every *one* of 'em doesn't have some crippling *deformity*, you can't even *apply* for this thing unless you're hooked up to some kind of *machine*. The couple that can actually *feed* themselves are considered the Brains of the oper*ation*, like the cumulative IQ of the entire *box* of 'em adds up to: Maybe we'll let you out of the *house* once in a while.)

Jack   These are the ones who hate you.

Robert   They *despise* me, Jack, like a pack of *dogs*, they wanna *eat* me, these people.

Jack   Why?

Robert   My *motivation*! The Fat Schmuck is constantly *harping* on my supposed *motivation*, like first he reads my *mind* –

Jack   Then he takes a pause.

Robert   To *stroke* himself and then he whispers my twisted thoughts into the *ears* of these *freaks* which is like (all kidding aside here), there's a real thing of like: If the freaks *believe* this guy, then that's pretty much what *happens* to me, the whole *system* comes down to: Can the Fat Schmuck *convince* these people.

Jack   You think he can.

Robert   You should *hear* him.

Jack   Pretty convincing.

Robert   Makes Pontius Pilate look like he wasn't *trying*.

Jack   Guy's good.

Robert   He's *whispering*, *out*lining my particular *motivation*, like I'm a very specific *kind* of sociopath.

Jack   Like he's a shrink.

Robert   Like he's a *scientist*.

Jack   Oh, man.

Robert   The *airtightness* he's got going.

Jack   He's good, this guy.

Robert   Like I'm such a freaking *socio*path, it's so completely *proven*, it's like how could I *not* do this thing.

Jack   But which you didn't do.

Robert   But which I didn't exactly *do*!

Jack   (Whoa whoa whoa whoa.)

Robert   The *science*, Jack.

Jack   Whoa, Bob.

Robert   He's got the science *doing* the *accusing* –

Jack   *Bob*.

Pause.

Robert   What.

Jack   Which is it here?

Robert   Which is what?

Jack   Bobby: which is it.

Robert   Oh, come *on*, Jack, for Chris*SAKE*!

Jack   You didn't *exactly*?

Pause.

Did not exactly? Is that what this is now?

Pause.

Robert   Don't you turn on me, Jack.

Jack   What did you do *exactly*, Bob?

Robert   I'm warning you.

Jack (*calmly*)   You're warning me?

Robert   I'm *begging* you, OK?

Jack   Why don't you tell me about it.

Robert   It was *justified*.

Jack   You've got a pretty subjective view of what –

Robert   DON'T TELL ME WHAT I HAVE DONE.
DON'T TELL ME WHAT I HAVE.

Jack   Take it easy, now.

Robert   How is it half the world can read your *mind* all of
a sudden? One day you wake up *transparent*? You spend your
whole previous *life* trying to get someone to understand half
a *sentence* of what you're *thinking* and then all of a sudden
you're completely *see-through* and every prosecuting *crack* and
every Faithless Fucking Long Lost Brother can parse your
exact views of *justice*.

Jack   You calm down now, Bobby.

Robert   Based on the, like, EVIDENCE piled up from
Not Being Here a Single *Second* IN HALF A LIFETIME.

Jack   Bobby, you take it easy now before I get up.

He is seated at the table. He looks evenly at **Robert**. *Pause. Like a
previously enraged, now whipped dog,* **Robert** *sits on the floor.
Pause.* **Jack** *stands, carries the bourbon to* **Robert**.

Jack (*offering the bottle*)   Let's see you do some work on that.

Robert (*upset*)   Christ, Jack.

Jack (*offering the bottle, sympathetically*)   All right.

Robert   I gotta be afraid of you now?

Jack   No.

Robert   You're gonna hurt me now all of a sudden?

Jack   I'm not gonna hurt you.

Robert   You hate me?

Jack   You know I don't.

Robert (*not rhetorically*)   How do I know that?

Pause.

Don't know how I would know that, Jack.

Jack   You're right.

Robert   Not sure exactly where I'd get that from.

Jack   I don't hate you, Bob.

Robert (*taking the bottle*)   (Jesus.)

Jack   I apologize.

Robert   I can't tell who's out to get me, Jack, and based on *lately*, it's just about everybody.

Jack   I'm not out to get you.

Robert (*drinks, then*)   (Damn.)

Jack (*like a kindly nurse*)   Why don't you take one more level out of that thing, see if that helps at all.

Robert (*like a child*)   Burning my stomach.

Jack   Your stomach bothering you?

Robert   A little.

Jack   Let's try one more out of that mother, see if we can calm that stomach down some.

Robert   All right. (*He drinks.*)

Jack   There you go.

Robert (*re: his bourbon intake*)   I did as much as I could.

Jack   You did fine.

Robert   You want some?

Jack   Sure.

Robert (*as* **Jack** *drinks*)   There's whole Theories, Jack, stating, like, Who even *knows*.

Jack   Subjectivity.

Robert   There's guys who teach this stuff full-*time*: That you can't actually *say*.

Jack   Objectively.

Robert   There's no actual way to say for sure what happened, most of the time.

Jack (*checking with him*)   You did it.

Robert   That's not the point.

Jack   You did it, Bob.

Robert   Some of this stuff, how are you supposed to argue with this crap?

Jack   Facts.

Robert   However you wanna put it.

Jack   Evidence.

Robert   But what I was *thinking* at the *time*, my particular *reasons*.

Jack (*helping* **Robert**)   How would he know that.

Robert   A person can't, like, *divine* my *thinking*, Jack.

Jack   He's putting words in your mouth.

Robert   He's putting words in my *mind*.

Jack   Mmm.

Robert   They *all* are, the news*papers*, I'm not *like* that. I don't even *look* like that picture they got, *you* saw the thing. Do I even *look* like that?

Pause.

You think maybe Daddy saw that picture in the paper anywhere?

Pause.

Am I as big as him?

Pause.

There's still some soaps and stuff, some hair cream back there that smells exactly like him, back in the can, if you wanna get a whiff.

Pause.

You remember that time I got bitten by that animal? (*Beat.*) 'Member that?

Jack (*softly*)   Yeah.

Robert   'Member that time?

Jack   I do, yeah.

Robert   I was asleep.

Jack   Sound asleep, the thing bit your face.

Robert   Remember that?

Jack   You had that red mark on your cheek that whole summer.

Robert   What *was* that that got me, you think?

Jack   I don't know.

Robert   It hurt.

Jack   You ended up bleeding a lot, yeah.

Robert   It was dark.

Jack   Sure.

Robert (*a confession*)   I cried a lot, Jack.

Pause.

I couldn't stop crying.

Jack   Middle of the night, Bob, thing must've scared you half out of your mind.

Robert (*apologizing*)   I couldn't stop screaming, I remember.

Jack (*sympathetically*)   It bit you on the *face*.

Robert   You know what?

Jack (*defending him*)   You were six years old.

Robert   I wonder if it didn't even *bite* me? I always suspected that, that maybe it just ran *across* me. I always sort of thought that.

Jack   *Still*, Jesus Christ.

Robert   My *throat*, I remember, from the *screaming*.

Jack   A rat ran across your *face*, Bobby.

Robert   A rat?

Jack   *Something*.

Robert   I always pictured like a demon.

Jack   A demon?

Robert   Just Nails and Hair and *Breath*.

Jack   So no wonder.

Robert   Once I started screaming, Jack, it kept coming.

Jack   You were *six*.

Robert   I couldn't *stop* it.

Jack   It's understandable.

Robert   We didn't want him to come in.

Pause.

We heard him moving around, I remember, and we didn't want him to have to come in. (*Beat.*) 'Could I stop crying,' you said, 'Could I try to keep it *down* a little?' and I tried, I Remember Trying, but it took me over, it had a *hold* of me, Jackson, I couldn't stop screaming. 'Will You Quiet *Down* in there!' (*Beat.*) From the kitchen. From in here. 'Will You Two Quiet *Down*.'

Pause.

(*Whispering*.) But 'Is it under the bed? It's in here somewhere, did you just *hear* that? There's a *demon* who *tasted* me, Jackie, Where *is* it?'

Jack   Bobby, come on.

Robert   I tried to Shut Up, but the more I *tried* to, the more I couldn't Shut Up.

Jack   There's no *thing* here –

Robert   We heard him get up. The chair scrapes on the floor. He stands up.

Beat.

Oh Christ, I thought, oh Jesus, here it comes. 'Just please shut up now,' you said, 'Just *please*, Bobby, be *quiet* now.' But I *couldn't*, though. I couldn't stop screaming, and now he's *coming*. Here he *comes*, Jackie, *Hide* Me.

Pause.

But Jack? Here's what I remember. (Me crying and the blood, and my throat, and here he comes.) But this is what I remember: he came in and he stood there.

Beat.

He didn't turn the light on. He stood there, in the dark. I was crying and he stood at the end of the bed. He didn't say anything. (*Beat.*) I was looking at him, peeking up at him and after a while I could *hear* him, breathing. I could hear him 'cause I had stopped crying. And then . . . (Remember this?) Then he stayed there. In our room. The three of us, in the dark. He was watching us. Just standing there quietly watching us. Until we fell asleep.

Pause.

Jack   Except we weren't asleep.

Robert   He thought we were.

Jack   Oh, Bob.

Robert   And only then he went out, I remember. *After* we were OK.

Jack   You weren't OK.

Robert   He thought I was.

Jack   You started to cry as soon as he turned his back and you never stopped. You cried until it got light.

Robert   Quietly, though.

Jack   You wet the *bed*.

Robert   I was scared.

Jack   That's my *point*.

Robert (*defending the father*)   He came in and stood there.

Jack   You had a *gash* on your *face*.

Robert   He didn't *know* that.

Jack (*fiercely, an outburst*)   You were Six Years Old. So What. You *Disturbed* him? He was kind enough to not *Attack* You?

Beat.

Robert   He didn't leave until it was time to go, Jack.

Jack (*with disgust*)   Oh, you gotta be kidding me.

Robert   He waited 'til it was OK.

Jack   What are you saying, *generally* this is? You have a little *fable* constructed?

Robert   It's true.

Jack   That what. He had a *plan* for you?

Robert   He waited 'til we were OK.

Jack   He *waited*? When he left? You were *seven*.

Robert   I was all right.

Jack   You were all right.

Robert   I was fine.

Jack   Tell me how all right this is: which part's OK, the nightmares? (Do you sleep, now? Have you *ever* slept through the night?)

Robert   I don't need much.

Jack   (I see.) Your Average kid, Bobby. (This might be news to you.) Most kids are *hungry* every once in a while. Most kids you don't *always* have to *beg* them to *eat*, to keep them from dis*appearing*. (You were Not All Right, Bobby, You were not *fine*.)

Beat.

Robert   So maybe he overestimated me.

Jack (*beat*)   (That is so *unspeakably* –) What's the fable? What do you think? (Because it's *delusional*.) What, you think he *noticed* you? He didn't *like* you, Bob.

Pause. **Robert** *is wounded.*

Robert   Why would you say that?

Pause.

You can be a real bastard, you know that? Sometimes you have a guy who doesn't talk all that much but then he does and he sticks some sentence right in your *eye*, Jack.

Jack   He didn't see your picture in the paper.

Robert   You know what you are? Is Who can tell if you're gonna suddenly turn on a relative, Jack, Christ.

Jack   I didn't turn on you.

Robert   Whatever you did.

Jack   I wouldn't turn on you.

Robert   I guess one guy's turning on somebody is another guy's punching me in the throat.

Jack   Those are my choices?

Robert   You know what I'm saying.

Jack   Those are the same thing.

Robert   You Know What I'm *SAYING*, JACK.

Pause. **Robert** *will forgive.*

Jack   I'm sorry.

Robert   (Jesus.)

Jack   I apologize.

Pause.

Robert   (Fucking *hot* in here, Jack. It gets hot in here with you around.)

Jack   (It's not always like this?)

Robert   (It's never like this.)

Jack   (Really.)

Robert   (I'm the only guy *around*, for one thing.)

Jack   (Does seem a little tight.)

Robert   (Jangles the nerves, you and me in the same *room*, it's enough to get the *nerves* jangled.)

Jack   (Does seem so.)

Robert   (Probably one of those blood deals.)

Jack   (Probably.)

Robert   (That thing about if a horse and a donkey get together you get an ass or something but the thing can't have its own kids.)

Jack (*beat*)   Do people usually know what you're saying, Bob?

Robert   No. Not usually.

Jack   Yeah.

Robert   I usually would've already stopped trying by now, if it was somebody else.

Jack   I'll take that as a compliment.

Robert (*allowing it to be a compliment*)   . . . OK.

Pause.

Jack (*a conciliatory offer*)   You wanna beer?

Robert   You gonna get it?

Jack   Sure.

Robert   I thought you had a pretty solid prejudice built up.

Jack   I was gonna find a rag or something.

Robert (*standing*)   I'll do it.

Jack   Really?

Robert   Not everyone is afraid of a little *odor*, Jack.

Jack   Is that right.

Robert   Certain guys, a fridge makes 'em *brave*.

Jack   You know the saying: Courage and stupid are pretty close relatives.

Robert   That's not a saying.

Jack   Yeah, well.

Robert (*crossing to the fridge*)   There's a technique, Jack. It's a thing of being quick.

Jack   It *smells* in there, is what it's a thing of.

Robert   Takes some aggression.

Jack   A smell wants to get *out*, Bob. A smell is in a *hurry*.

Robert   That's what I'm saying.

Jack   So let's see it, then.

Robert *opens the refrigerator deftly, removes beers, closes it.*

Robert (*with some pride*)   Anybody's eyes tearing?

Jack (*re: the number of beers*)   You only got two.

Robert   I only *need* to get two, due to my expertise.
(*Tossing a beer to* **Jack**.) Coming.

They drink needfully. Pause. A deep breath.

In olden times, Jack, with the whole tar and feather
scenario? At least eventually you can peel it off you.

Jack   Excuse me?

Robert   You gotta figure it *hardens*, over time. Once it
dries you can scrape it off, wouldn't you think?

Jack   I guess.

Robert   So OK, that would be fine, back then you take
your medicine, except but now half the population carries
weapons, you can't exactly peel it off when someone shoots
you in the neck.

Jack   You think someone wants to shoot you?

Robert   There's people who honestly hate me.

Jack   Who?

Robert   *Everybody*. The way the Fat Schmuck portrays it?
I'm like a Social Piranha. If I had a gun and they saw me on
the street? Do the world a *favor*.

Jack   Do you have a gun?

Robert   Do you think I should have one?

Jack   You don't have one.

Robert   I can't like, *purchase* things, Jack, I'm not exactly a
consumer.

Jack   You don't have a gun.

Robert (*alluding to the environs*)   You're *looking* at it. I don't *prefer* the like, *style* of this existence.

Jack   You didn't buy a gun.

Robert   With an arms dealer type, a lot of these guys? you offer the kitchen *table* in a *barter* deal? they laugh you out of the *room*.

Jack   Hypothetically.

Robert   I *tried* it.

Jack   How'd you meet an arms dealer?

Robert   'You'd hafta *pay* me to haul that shit outta here,' that's the kind of response.

Jack   This happened?

Robert   I can work a shovel, Jack, I can do your driveway, but it has to *snow*, and if it doesn't happen to be *winter*, well, let's just say I haven't had a lot of *work* lately, so I'm not coming from a position of *strength* over here, pretty much *anybody* at any time, they say Take it or Leave it. What are my options?

Jack   How do you mean?

Robert   I mean I don't *have* any, Jack, is what I *mean* is that some Asswipe comes up with like, a half a dozen *String* Beans, and how about we trade this for everything you *Have*, I don't have a lot of *Choice*, Whatever he *Wants*, 'cause if I don't get the *Food*, there's a very serious thing of: Are you actually gonna *starve* to *death* out here.

Jack   You're broke.

Robert   I haven't had a lot of work lately.

Jack   What's lately?

Robert   Well, it stretches out to pretty much *Ever*, so when somebody says there's an option for Twenty *Dollars*, it's a fairly weak position when the first thing you think of is how much *Spaghettios* that would add up to.

Jack   This is what happened.

Robert   Here's what a Weak Position is, Jack, here's like, what a weak position *is*, OK? You're walking, you're *going* somewhere, right? which is *fine*, so far so *good*, but say *suddenly* (and for no reason any observer could even *conceive* of), say you Turn *Around*.

Jack   This is you.

Robert   You spin *around* one-eighty, you go right back where you *came* from.

Jack   Why'd you do that?

Robert   No apparent *reason*.

Jack (*not appreciating the import*)   You turned around.

Robert   Like a *moron*! like who's the *patient*, Jack, who let that guy *out*?

Jack (*an attempt to understand*)   You were walking.

Robert   It was really *hot* that day, I figured: Go for a swim, right?

Jack   All right.

Robert   Right?

Jack   Makes sense.

Robert   But you gotta walk *down* there, is the *thing*, and if you're as hot as *I* am, Jack? It gets *internal*, you can't just stand under a *hose*, you need something *deep*, you gotta jump off a *rock* into something *Arctic, you gotta go all the way to* Eifert's, which is I don't even *know* what, it's *miles*.

Jack   (Is that still there?)

Robert   And it's still about a couple Dozen *Miles*.

Jack   You went down for a swim.

Robert But you just get hotter every *step*, turns out it's the total *opposite* of your goal you set up.

Jack To what, to cool off?

Robert You just get *Hotter*.

Jack So you turn around.

Robert Like a *Dip*shit.

Jack Well, that happens though, Bob.

Robert Not when somebody's *Looking* at you. Not when the guy is *Spying* on you, forming an extremely unflattering initial *Impression*.

Jack Somebody saw you.

Robert Sees me *Stopping*, for crying out loud, and then turning *around*, imagine what he's *Thinking*!

Jack He saw you on the road there.

Robert Like what am I, A Fucking *Oakie*? 'Hey, look, it's a Peasant, take a *Picture*, Oh my heavens, *look*, it turned *around*, Stop the *Car*.'

Jack Somebody offered you a ride.

Robert If you wanna *call* it that.

Jack What else would you call it?

Robert (*emphatically*) Jack. You don't just get *into* one of these things. It's not like it's a *car*, you get in*side*. You gotta *climb* up the *side* of the thing, there's like, *Stairs*, you gotta *scale*, like it's a freaking *Altar* of some kind.

Jack It's a big car.

Robert You're a *pilgrim*.

Jack You have to climb up to get in.

Robert And say you do manage to hoist yourself up into the bastard?

Jack   You did, right?

Robert   It *Knows*, Jack. By Instinct, the thing *knows* you're not One of Them. It's like, *programmed* to Recognize, in the *seats*, the thing has Ass Sensors and say you have the bony ass of an *Oakie*? (And this is true.) You sit *down*, the thing *Automatically Despises* you.

Jack   You got in the car.

Robert   (*beat*)   I *What*?

Jack   Is that what happened?

Robert   That's how you *See* this?

Jack   I'm asking.

Robert   Jesus *Christ*.

Jack   *What*.

Robert   You ever see a Grown Man in *Shorts*?

Jack   (Is that a real question?)

Robert   I'm climbing up into the guy's Personal Rolling *Bank*, I'm coming up over the like, *Horizon* and I see this guy's *Legs*. (You ever see something Peeled that wasn't supposed to be? Something that got Boiled, over*night*, that was only supposed to be Heated Up?) He's Wearing *Shorts*!

Jack (*repulsed*)   That's disgusting.

Robert   And he's sitting there, and the *Exertion* of sitting on his *ass* in his *Shorts*, is causing the legs to *Jiggle*! They're Jiggling and like, *Pulsating*, like his skin is just chock-full of *Shit*. (I'm telling you, it was all I could *do* to not Throw Up all over his Air Conditioning.)

Jack   You threw up on him?

Robert   Well, I haven't exactly *eaten*, so what comes out is more of a *Burp* thing. There I am, the *sight* of this guy and the first thing out of my *mouth* is this half-retch *Burp*.

Jack (*sympathetically*)   (Oh, man.)

Robert   Which, you know what he *says* at this point? I swear to *God*, you know how the guy *responds*? (*Beat*.) He says, 'Oops.'

Jack   He said oops?

Robert   Out of *Sympathy*! Out of like, Oh that *Happens* (whenever someone gets a faceful of my hairless jiggling shit-filled *Legs*), 'Oops,' this is what comes out of his *Mouth* for the love of *God*, '*Oops*.' Jack, Who *Are* These People?

Jack   'Oops'?

Robert   Where does that *come* from?

Jack   I don't know.

Robert   And then it doesn't *Stop*, though.

Jack   What?

Robert   With the Bizarre Commentary.

Jack   He's got more?

Robert   'Do You Want to Pick Some *Music*?'

Jack   You're kidding.

Robert   'Would you like to pick some *MUSIC*?'

Jack   He *said* that?

Robert   WHO *ARE* THESE PEOPLE?

Jack   You almost just *puked* on the guy.

Robert   And he's got, like, a Whole *Collection* of *Chins*. He Turns his *Head* and I swear to God, there's a little *Delay* before all the Chins Catch *Up*, before they fall in Line. The guy *Turns* to me. (Each one of his chins, Jack, what does that *Cost*, To Develop A *Collection* of those things?)

Jack   Over a lifetime.

Robert   A *Fortune*.

Jack   Millions.

Robert   And so when the guy *turns* to me, I'm *lost* in trying to figure out how much it'd be to *feed* the chins, the *housing* costs, I'm into the horrible *math* of the thing and he goes *Broadside* with this *Invitation*.

Jack   You shoulda gotten outta the car, Bob.

Robert   Did I want to Pick Some *Music*!

Jack   Shoulda got out of the car.

Robert   I WAS HUNGRY.

Pause.

There's no knobs, Jack. There's no, like, Tapes on this thing. I'm not a Moron, I do *fine*, I can *operate* your average *machine*. But there's barely any *buttons*.

Jack   The radio.

Robert   I'm about to kick the thing to *death* trying to get it to make some *sounds*, I'm looking around for something *sharp*, I'd like to ram a Rusty Spike right up under the *rewind* button, and the guy (*again!*), like he has a *Hobby* of saying the *least* Appropriate Thing, like he's a *collector* of Stupidity, I'm Attacking his *Dashboard*.

Jack   What's he say?

Robert   I'm using both hands and a *Foot*, Jack.

Jack   What's he say?

Robert   I'm *Sweating* from the *beating* I'm giving to his *Radio*.

Jack   What's he say.

Robert   'Do you ever do odd *Jobs*?'!

Beat.

Jack   (Are you serious?)

Robert   ('So, do you ever do odd jobs?')

Jack   (Jesus Christ.)

Robert   His *chins*, Jack and the *Math* and his *Shorts*, I'm practically *Hallucinating* from how *Awful* this guy is.

Jack   'Do you ever do odd *jobs*?'

Robert   I'm using the flat of my hand on his *eject* button.

Jack   You got out of the car.

Robert   My *Position*, Jack.

Jack   You got out of the *car*.

Robert   What *Choice* do I have?

Jack   You've *got* one, you get *out*, Bobby.

Robert   I'm like *Prostrate* for the guy *already*, my position is *incredibly* Weak, and plus I'm *thrown* because How Does a Guy Like This *Exist*, even (it just came *out*, Jack), 'Do I ever do odd jobs?'

Jack (*anticipating what's coming, dreading it*)   (Oh, Bob.)

Robert   I say –

Jack   (Oh, Bob, come on.)

Robert   I say, 'Sometimes. Half up front.'

Pause.

Robert (*asking, quietly*)   (Why'd I say that, Jack?)

Jack   (What'd he want you to do?)

Robert   (Why did I say that?)

Jack (*supportively*)   (You were hungry.)

Robert   (Was I *that* hungry?)

Jack   (You hadn't eaten in who knows how long.)

Robert   (What won't I do?)

Jack   (What did he want?)

Robert   (I didn't know.)

Jack   (You what?)

Robert   (I didn't know what he wanted.)

Jack   (You said sometimes?)

Robert (*ashamed*)   (Yeah. I said Half up front.)

Jack   (Oh, Bobby.)

Robert   (I didn't *care* what he wanted, Jack. I was . . . I was *desperate* to trans*act* with the guy. For some reason? Even with the world's *worst* guy sitting there, all I wanted [I couldn't *help* it, like I caught a *disease*] I was suddenly *Aching* to *Transact* with this man.)

Pause.

(*Quietly, and with a kind of amazement.*) He takes out his Wallet. (He's smiling at me like we're in on something.) He takes out his Wallet, this loaf of *bread*, this Loaf, and he pulls out a Twenty. (*Beat. then, wondrously.*) A twenty-dollar bill. He holds it up, up by his face (he's *grinning*) and I'm Transfixed by the thing. I'm Mesmerized by the bill, Jack, and Suddenly: He's holding a *treat*. He's holding a *snack*, he's a big *kid* and I'm his *Dog*, But now he's a fat *child* holding a *Hammer* and I'm *panting*, I'm *salivating*, staring up at the thing: Will I Roll Over? Will I *Heel*? Will I Do Him This *Kindness*? (*Beat.*) It's not Transacting now, Jackson. You wanna know what it is now? Honestly? I want him gone. All I want in the world is for the fat child to go away. I reach out for the twenty, but I go right past it. I Open his Door. (*Beat.*) We're doing fifty, *easily*, and his door is wide Open. (*Beat.*) The guy doesn't *react*. He's holding the twenty, up in the air, still smiling at me, like am I gonna Fetch, but his *door* is wide *Open*, like he hasn't had an *instinct* since *birth*, like he pays somebody to *wipe* him, Jack. I reach under his legs. (*Beat.*) Both hands, I touch his Ass and his Legs and I tip him out. I tip him over, out the open door. He's light. There's no sound. (*Beat.*) Like

he gets sucked up the Chimney. Blank. He just all of a
sudden isn't there anymore.

Pause.

Jack   Is he dead?

Robert   I climb over, I drive the car, run out of gas in
some state, I can't remember. I sit there until people come
and drag me out.

Pause.

Jack   Is he dead?

Robert   He broke his neck. And one of his arms is in bad
shape. His back.

Jack   He's alive.

Robert   Yeah.

Beat.

Jack   What're the charges?

Robert   You name it.

Pause.

He wanted me to clean his bathroom.

Pause.

Jack   That was the job.

Robert (*without rancour*)   Guy picks me up on the road,
Would I clean his bathroom. Would I come to his house. A
kindness, would I clean his bathroom.

Pause.

His name is Tom. That's the guy's name, apparently.

Pause.

I did it, Jack.

Pause.

The way he says it happened? That's pretty much what happened.

Pause.

I had to give up the house. (*Beat.*) The bail guy, he said he'd put up the whole thing if I let him have the house, Jack.

Jack   That's all right.

Robert   He did say I can stay here though, until it's over.

Pause.

I figure we can leave a sign up, just in case anybody . . .

Jack   It doesn't matter, Bob.

Pause.

Robert (*quietly*)   Hey, Jackie?

Jack   Yeah.

Robert   What are they gonna do to me?

Jack   I don't know.

Robert   They hate me.

Jack   Yeah.

Robert   If they had their way . . . My feeling is they want me dead.

Jack   That's possible.

Robert   And why wouldn't they get their way?

Jack *has no answer. Pause.* **Robert** *kneels.*

Robert   I can only remember the beginning, I think I've got the beginning pretty much down.

Jack   What're you doing.

Robert (*an invitation to join him in prayer*)   Can you give me a hand here, Jack?

Jack   Oh, Bobby, come on.

Robert   Bless Daddy and Jackson and God bless our
Mother, up in heaven, full of grace, . . . hollow be her name
. . . (up in heaven, Full of grace).

Beat.

That's where I dry out.

Jack   Bobby, get up, all right?

Robert   What's that next bit, d'you have any idea?

Jack   No.

Robert   There's that middle part where she and God
watch you sleeping, what's that part.

Jack   I don't remember.

Robert   You don't remember praying?

Jack (*lying*)   . . . No. I don't remember anything.

Pause.

Robert (*still kneeling*)   Will you help me, Jack?

Pause.

Will you pray with me?

Jack   I'm not gonna pray with you, Bob, no.

Robert   Why?

Jack   . . . I don't know.

Robert (*still kneeling*)   Then can we go now?

Pause. He stands.

Jack? Is it time to go now?

Jack   Bob –

Robert   Can we get out of here?

Jack   I'm not going anywhere.

Pause.

Robert   Excuse me?

Jack   I'm not gonna go anywhere.

Robert   You're not gonna go anywhere.

Jack   No.

Robert (*beat*)   But you're not staying, though. You keep saying how there's no chance you're staying.

Jack   I'm not staying.

Robert   So how's that *work* then?

Pause.

Not sure how that's possible. How's that possible, Jack?

Jack   I'm not here to help you, Bob. (*Beat.*) I'm not gonna pray and I'm not gonna rescue anybody. I'm not going anywhere.

Pause.

Robert   So . . . So then what're you *doing* here?

Pause. **Robert** *looks once, quickly, to the paper bag which* **Jack** *left on the counter in the opening moments.*

(*With mounting suspicion.*) You thought you'd drop by, bring the brother a sandwich, have a conver*sation*. (*Beat.*) Jack? What're You *Doing* Here?

Pause. Then **Robert** *moves to the counter. He looks inside the bag. He reaches into the bag, and without removing it, he fires the gun which is inside. Bang.*

Lights out.

Act Two

Moments later. **Robert** *points a pistol.* **Jack** *sits at the table.*

Robert   Put Your Hands Up.

Jack (*reasonably*)   That's loaded, Bob.

Robert   Put Your *Hands* Up!

Jack   I'm not putting my hands up.

Robert   You Know What I Should Do?

Jack   Will you be careful with that please?

Robert   You know what a *sane* person does right now?

Jack   Bob.

Robert   (Let's not forget who is currently holding a Weapon over here, Jack, let's *Remind* ourselves, before we start with the 'Bob' shit, let's remember who's pointing what at *who* here.)

Jack (*standing*)   You want a beer?

Robert   *Eat* me.

Jack (*to himself*)   (Take that as a yes.)

Robert   What a *Sane* person *Does* right now, Anyone with half a sense of Right and Wrong, they Shoot you in the *head*.

Jack (*regarding the refrigerator, to himself*)   (All right, courage.)

Robert   You know what's hideous?

Jack   Besides the smell in this thing?

Jack *opens the refrigerator, removes two beers, closes it quickly.*

Robert   Is not only do you *Drive* a Great Distance to Kill me –

Jack (*re: the smell*)   (*Man.*)

Robert   Which, that Alone, is *Astonishing*.

Jack (*re: the smell*)   (*Wow.*)

Robert   But then you show up under the like, *Guise* of 'How've you *been*!' You come in *Costume*! 'Great to *see* you!' 'I really *missed* you!'

Jack   I never said that.

Robert   So *What*!

Jack (*tossing a beer to* **Robert**)   Comin'.

Robert (*catching it*)   (And don't be so sure there's not some poison fungus on the lid of that thing, by the way.)

Jack   (Thanks.)

Robert   You know what else? Next time you're out to Assassinate your own *Brother*?

Jack   Is that what I'm doing?

Robert   Next time you're out to *fool* your Profoundly *Stupid* little brother into thinking you've got a Decent Bone in your fucking *Body*, I have an Idea for you.

Jack   What's that.

Robert   WHY BOTHER!

Jack (*not following*)   (I think I lost you.)

Robert   What's the Point, Jack, Jesus Christ, out of, like, *Pleasure*. (I've *seen* this, I've seen a cat half murder a bird and then carry the thing around in its *mouth* for half a day, just gentle enough to not send a tooth right through its *heart*.) First we get in a *Conversation*! First you get me kissing your *ass* halfway to the *Moon* for God's sake: Have a *Beer*. (Who said you could have that by the way?) Take a *Shower*, *Stay* a while, and oh, here's some like, deep confessions, some personal *confidences* regarding my tortured fucking Mental State.

Jack (*re:* **Robert**'s *tirade*)   You finished?

Robert No.

Jack All right.

Robert And you *shut* up.

Jack (*offering the bourbon*) Take some of this, Bob.

Robert (*accepting the bottle*) Which is another thing, you psychopath, What is it? You have a thing of shooting drunk guys? I'm a fatted calf? Any assassin worth his *weight*, Jack, he doesn't waste half a bottle of good bourbon and any *number* of beers on what's about to be a *corpse*.

Jack Where'd you hear that?

Robert DON'T ASK ME QUESTIONS.

Jack (Sorry, Jesus.)

Robert (*quoting* **Jack**) 'Are you *Hungry*!'

Jack That I said.

Robert 'Can I make you an *Omelette*!'

Jack If you had an egg, maybe.

Robert 'How about a *Sandwich*!' (Of all the things to offer a half-*starved* person, nourishment! You need some *help*.)

Jack Hah.

Robert (*re: the sandwich*) And *then*: (Here's where it's Insidious, where a sane person puts you out of your twisted *Misery*) It's Not A Sandwich!

Jack It's a weapon.

Robert It's a *gun*.

Jack A gun, right, sorry.

Robert (And you know what else? This Blasé thing you've got going here with the Who cares if he's got the gun thing is *Not* working, whatever it's supposed to be *doing* it's not *doing* it, whatever they *teach* you in Assassin class, you

can *forget* it, 'cause as soon as I've finished saying this, I'm
going to fire this thing, I don't care if you act scared or not.)

Jack   When might that *be*, you think?

Robert (*re: the blaséness*)   It's not Working, Jack.

Jack   Seems like you might go on for a while.

Robert (*pointing the gun at* **Jack**)   All right.

Jack   My life expectancy is through the roof.

Robert (*aiming*)   Don't move.

Pause. **Jack** *appears nonplussed.*

Jack   I'm not moving, Bob.

Robert   Why aren't you?

Jack   Why aren't I?

Robert *fires into the ceiling. Bang.*

Jack   You know, that just made a *hole* right there.

Robert (*disconcerted by* **Jack**'s *lack of fear*)   What kind of
Lunatic Are You? *Honestly.* What's *Wrong* with you? I'm
Serious, one of these minutes I'm gonna shoot you with this
thing.

Jack   Bob.

Robert (*sadly*)   You know what it's *like* around here? I have
watched television, I have *seen* Brochures, It is *impossible* to not
All the *Time* be thinking about how other people have *Lives*,
Jack. Other people *talk* to people. (There's people out there
that all they *do* is *Talk* to one another.) And there's *me*, who
all I ever do, every *day* for the last twenty-three* *years* and
two months and I don't give a shit how many days, exactly,
all I do is *wonder* if there's a *chance* one of the two of you
bastards is gonna come *Home* soon.

---

* This number may be adjusted, based on the age of the actors.

Jack   Well, I'm sorry about that.

Robert   (Do you know what it's like to have your dream come true show up with a Gun?) (*Beat.*) IT'S A DISAPPOINTMENT!

Jack   Bob.

Robert   (If one more time you use my name, Jack, I'm gonna Wreak Havoc, I swear to God.)

Jack   Can I say something here?

Robert   You saved my *life*, you prick.

Jack   I never saved your life.

Robert   I would've *died*.

Jack   You were about six feet off the ground.

Robert   *Sixty*, more like.

Jack   Who told you that?

Robert   You Saved My Life.

Jack   It never happened.

Robert   I fell and you caught me, all right? There's some Facts if there ever were any.

Jack   You landed on me.

Robert   Bullshit.

Jack   I was surprised, Bob, you landed on my head. I was irritated.

Robert   That's a Lie.

Jack   Plus that tree was only ten feet *total*.

Robert   You Got the Wrong Tree.

Jack   It's the only one out there.

Robert   Shut up.

Jack Fine.

Robert That's not even what we're talking about.

Jack What're we talking about?

Robert We're talking about Where's your sense of Decency?

Jack Ah.

Robert You were supposed to take *care* of me.

Jack Excuse me?

Robert That's what he told you.

Jack You *think* that?

Robert That was your *job*.

Jack No one ever said that.

Robert That was the *Understanding*.

Jack It might've worked *out* that way.

Robert So it wasn't Written *Down* anywhere. (How'd you get so Lawyer-ish all of a sudden? You Know Who You *Remind* Me Of?)

Jack He disappeared, Bob, there weren't any Instructions.

Robert So that's even *Sicker*.

Jack How is that sicker?

Robert You *Chose* to Raise me.

Jack Oh, I dunno. I just kept making breakfast.

Robert That's so *sick*, Jack, 'cause then *then* what? You half raise a guy and then you Abandon me to like, Gestate, before you decide to come back and *kill* me?

Jack Does that sound sensible?

Robert It's *insane*.

Jack   O*K* –

Robert   But to a Psychopath, to a *Maniac*, they don't exactly Employ *Logic*.

Jack (*an attempt to reason*)   You think what.

Robert   You're a *Freak*, is what I think.

Jack   Say I brought a gun.

Robert   You *did* bring a gun.

Jack   I brought a gun, OK.

Robert   Disguised as a sandwich, you sadist.

Jack   This means I'm gonna *kill* you?

Robert (*still holding the gun*)   Not anymore you're not.

Jack   Why would I want to kill you, Bob?

Robert   You saw the paper.

Jack   I don't read the paper.

Robert (*beat*)   You don't read the newspaper?

Jack   No.

Robert   You never *look* at the paper?

Jack   No.

Robert   (If you're lying to me, Jack, I don't *know* what, I'm gonna think of some way to Torture you.)

Jack   (Can you stop with the threats please?)

Robert   You didn't see my picture in the paper?

Jack   I never saw it in the paper.

Robert   So you heard it on the *radio*. (*Jesus*, Again with the hair-splitting lawyer shit.)

Jack   I don't listen to the radio.

Robert   You *what*?

Jack   I don't listen to the radio.

Robert   You were *driving*.

Jack   I never turn it on.

Robert   You don't drive with the *radio* on?

Jack   No.

Robert   *Why*?

Jack   I don't like it.

Robert   It's Not Whether you *Like* it or not, Jack, Christ, The Thing is right at Your *Fingertips*, You Turn it *On*.

Jack   I don't.

Robert   So the *Television*.

Jack   I don't watch it.

Robert   What's *Wrong* with You?

Jack   I never watch it, Bob. I don't like it.

Robert   So what, am I supposed to keep track of your freakish *Preferences* now? I have a list of your *Demented Tastes* tacked up somewhere?

Jack   Bob.

Robert   In case you stop by to *Kill* me I can make sure not to have any *Radios* on?

Jack (*evenly, re: the trial*)   I never heard about it.

Pause.

Robert   (Say that again.)

Jack   I didn't know about the trial. I didn't know it happened.

Pause.

Robert   You didn't know about it.

Jack   I'm not here to kill you, Bob. I'm not gonna kill you and I'm not gonna help you.

Pause. **Robert** *attempts to digest this.*

Robert   (You're not here to kill me.)

Jack   (No.)

Robert   (You didn't come here to Punish me?)

Jack   (No.)

Robert (*hurt, disappointed*)   (Why *not?*)

Jack   (Bob.)

Robert   (And you're not gonna Help me, Jackie?)

Jack   (I'm not gonna help you, no.)

Pause.

Robert   Hey, Jack?

Jack   Yeah.

Robert   Any way you might rethink that? Any chance you might give that one more thought? I'm in sort of a bad way.

Jack   I know that.

Robert   I don't wanna beg anybody.

Jack   I can't.

Robert   The Situation, it's sort of excruciating, the atmosphere around here is starting to wear me down a little.

Jack   I'm sorry.

Robert   I could use a hand.

Jack   I can't help you, Bobby. I can't help you.

Pause. Then **Robert** *attempts to pull a needle of hope from a haystack of despair.*

Robert (*quietly*)   You know what?

Jack   Why don't you sit down for a second?

Robert   (What time is it?)

Jack   I wanna explain something.

Robert (*hopefully*)   Your average paper? You know what I just realized? Your average Newspaper, it's not just the guy who Buys it, who Reads your typical paper.

Jack   Bob, please.

Robert (*with growing enthusiasm*)   You don't have to have a Subscription (I don't *think*), you don't have to be a *Citizen* to read a Newspaper.

Jack   I didn't *know* about it.

Robert   I'm not saying you did.

Jack   What *are* you saying.

Robert (*looking quickly to the door*)   (What Time is it?)

Jack   (Why.)

Robert   It's not like there's a Credit Check. A guy might be Blowing his Nose in the Crime Blotter, they don't like, Investigate, make sure you're *Liquid*, to sneeze into the *paper*.

Jack   What could that *mean*, Bob?

Robert   Correct me if I'm wrong.

Jack   OK.

Robert   You're not the only person on the *Planet*, contrary to the popular Thing. You're not here to help me? I have other *Options*. (And what is it: I'm not worth the *Trouble*? You can't turn on the *Television*? You can't be *Burdened with taking ten* Seconds to try and *rescue* me? Your fucking *Heart's* not in it?) Listen: *Listen*: I'm not like, *Dependent* on *You* to care enough, all right? You are *not* my only *Option*.

Pause.

(*Conversationally*.) (What time is it? People are creatures of habit, I don't know if you realize that.)

Jack   Bob.

Robert   (He'd get home around five, most nights, what time is it now?)

Jack   He's dead.

Pause.

He's Dead. He died.

Robert   . . . You don't know that.

Jack   I'll tell you what I know: He's not coming home, Bob, not ever.

Robert   Are you a bad person?

Jack   (He's gonna come to your Rescue? He's your Father?) He wouldn't Remember you. (He's not out there Thinking about you, Bobby, Christ, He's not *pining* after you.) He Didn't Like You. He Didn't Know You. (No One Can Help You. No One. No One Cares About You.)

Pause. **Robert** *still holds the gun.*

Robert (*quietly*)   (That's a fascinating comment there, Jack.) Oooh. (That is an interesting observation.)

Jack   He's not coming home, Bob. Not ever.

Pause. **Robert** *is despondent. He tosses the gun on to the table.*

Robert   Do what you want.

Beat. **Robert** *turns his back on* **Jack**.

Do what you want.

Jack   Bobby. (*Beat.*) Pick up the gun.

Robert *turns to face* **Jack**. *Beat.* **Jack** *picks up the gun, offers it to* **Robert**.

Jack   Take it.

Pause. **Jack** *holds the gun extended.*

Robert   You know what a sane person does right here?

Jack (*offering the pistol*)   Please.

Robert   He runs screaming.

Jack (*placing the gun back on the table. A decision to proceed*)   All right.

Robert   Right out the door screaming his head off. Gets as far away from you as there is.

Jack *sits at the kitchen table.*

Jack   Now listen a second. I'm gonna tell you something.

Robert   (There's an old saying, Jack: If you feel like you should run screaming? That's because you should.)

Jack (*simply – and he begins fondly*)   You were a fat kid. (*Beat.*) Fat. A fat child.

Pause.

Not chubby. Not plump, don't kid yourself: You were Fat.

Robert (*as he crosses to the door*)   (OK. You know what? You're out of your mind, Jack, keep the house.)

Jack *remains seated at the table, but he will lift the pistol. He fires it into the ceiling. Bang.* **Robert** *stops.* **Jack** *doesn't face* **Robert**.

Jack (*matter-of-factly, resignedly, sadly*)   (If you go, I'm gonna follow you right out the door.)

Pause. **Jack** *will hold the pistol.*

(*Again, fondly.*) You were born fat. Round, almost. A round baby and then a round little boy.

Beat.

Then this one morning, maybe six months after he left? You were messing around in there, I was yelling about hurry up, the bus is gonna come and you finally come out, you had this look on your face. You were sort of Stunned. (*Beat.*) Your clothes didn't fit. Like it Evaporated: you weren't fat anymore. You were a stick. You were a bone. That night I look over and I can see the veins in your temples. I watch you sleeping, and I can see the blood moving under your skin.

Pause.

I emptied my wallet, trying to get some food into you. You'd think a kid would respond to a bribe: You didn't. (*Beat.*) He was gone about a year, you turned eight and you started fainting. You were fainting at school all the time, the nurse would call, I'd tell her it runs in the family. (*Beat.*) (I was fifteen.) (*Beat.*) You know that dream? We're walking up on this cliff and it's windy and slippery, the two of us are up there and you're a little kid and you're messing around, you won't listen to me and I can tell it's about to happen and then you Fall. You slip out of my grasp and you fall off the edge. I see you falling through the air, falling, getting smaller and smaller, you Disappear.

Pause.

So I started talking. I told you all about the old man. Everything I could think of. I'd put some food in front of you, a glass of milk, a piece of bread. You'd listen like I was God talking and you'd eat whatever I put on a plate. Like you're munching popcorn, like I'm a movie. (*Beat.*) That was how it worked, a couple of years we did that. You would eat if I'd tell you everything I knew.

Pause.

Robert (*softly*)   I remember that. I remember us doing that.

Jack   I made it up, Bob.

Beat.

All of it. I made it all up. Everything I told you about him, every word was a lie.

Pause.

Robert   (How's this work now, what's the thing with this: You wanna *spook* me? What's the game. You trying to trick me into passing out? You want my *wallet*? I'm Fine, Jack.)

Jack   You might remember what he looked like, even that I don't know.

Robert   I remember who my father is.

Jack   A couple of things. The rat thing, I guess. You were young when he went.

Robert   I wasn't an infant.

Jack   You were seven. You were a baby.

Robert   I know what I know.

Jack   I'm sorry, Bob.

Robert   There's nothing to be *Sorry* about. What. You think you just *Erased* me? You think 'poof,' I'm an *Orphan* all of a sudden because You Happen to Levy some Weirdo Fucking *Proclamations*? You Think I *Believe* You?

Jack   I made it up. How he talked. How he slept, how he sneezed (that famous sneeze, the 'hi-*Ya*' sneeze).

Robert   I sneeze like that, Jack.

Jack   I made it up.

Robert   I *inherited* it. I *got* it from him.

Jack   The way he sat. The way he held your hand. His pipe. (He didn't smoke a pipe.)

Robert   So what stunk up the house, my *imagination*?

Jack   What he wore, his shoes, his skin, his Job. (He didn't drive a truck. I don't even know why I picked that.)

Robert   My father drove a truck.

Jack   He worked in an office.

Robert   Are you *joking*?

Jack   Right up there, two miles, maybe.

Robert   Is this a *routine*?

Jack   A shipping company, he was in charge of routes, or something, I dunno.

Robert   My father drove a logging truck.

Jack   You ever see any Logging Trucks around here anywhere? You ever in your *life see* an actual Logging Truck? What do they look like? (*Beat.*) He got home at five fifteen every night, that ever strike you as strange? For a guy who's off on a logging run God *knows* where, a place where they have *logs*, obviously. He makes it home from *Alaska* at five *fifteen* every night?

Pause.

Robert (*quietly*)   I'm not sure what your goal is here.

Jack   He's not ever coming back.

Robert   You don't know that.

Jack   I know it Absolutely.

Robert   He left under some Circumstances, Jack, and you may not (for some bizarro fucking Reason), you may not *choose* to Recall this, but there were some Factors.

Jack   He was average.

Robert   The ties that actually bind are made of, like, *nothing*, and when a beautiful woman drives up one morning there is some *pull* there, I don't care *how* you feel about a couple of *Children*, neither one of 'em sleeps in your Bed.

Jack   She didn't Exist.

Robert (*insisting on the myth*)   She wasn't a *Bumpkin*. This is no *Plough* horse, She had a head of *hair* this lady –

Jack   I never saw him *talk* to a woman. Not one time. At the store, he'd get his change in silence, Bob, with his head down. The checkout lady says have a nice day and he turns his back, he's *ashamed*. He couldn't *look* at *anyone*, let alone *speak*, he wasn't *capable*.

Robert (*stubbornly, from memory*)   The Old Man (and it's not all Positive, it's not like I have a Rosy Picture), the old man wasn't exactly *Reliable*.

Jack   He was predictable.

Robert   He and his friends, these are some Epic *Benders*.

Jack   He had a couple of beers a week.

Robert (*insistently*)   The old fart'd get *lost* coming home half the time, we'd have to get our flashlights and go get him, walk down to the local bar and fetch the old bastard.

Jack   How far is that, to Bert's, twenty miles? You were seven. We dragged our drunk father home twenty *miles*, Does that sound True to you?

Robert   We don't know where he *is*, Jack. (Think about this.) He blacks out for a week, he could end up *Anywhere*, with his Mind half *Fried*. He could be stumbling home right *now*, for all we know.

Jack (*an explosion*)   I MADE IT *UP*. Jesus Christ, Bobby, he was *NOTHING*. He was *AVERAGE*. I LIED TO YOU.

Pause.

His face, his shoes, his Reasons. (There was no Reason, Bobby, OK? There was no woman and no booze, he's not lost and there is no Reason.) I made it all up. Everything. I made up his Name. He doesn't *exist*, your father.

Pause. **Robert** *sits on the floor. A collapse.*

Robert   Are you a scientist?

Jack   You were fainting.

Robert   Am I an experiment?

Pause.

You made up his name? Jack? What's his name?

Jack   His name was Don.

Pause.

Robert   His name was Don. (*Beat.*) (At bedtime, they tell you about Santa. The next day they sit you down, confidentially, they let you in a little secret.)

Jack   They were stories, Bobby. They were fables.

Robert   (Fables.) Jack: I was eight years old. I was a *child*. I *believed* in fables.

Jack   What are you now, Bob? Are you a child now?

Pause.

You wanna hear a Story? You wanna hear a True one?

Pause.

Couple of kids get home from school one day. It's raining. They're stuck inside, passing time. They wrestle, they fight. The little one cries, the big one says he's sorry, couple hundred games of crazy eights. They're waiting for their father to get home. (*Beat.*) After a hundred years, it's five fifteen. His car pulls into the driveway. The little one runs to the window, sticks his forehead on the glass. The older one is fourteen, you'd think he wouldn't, but he can't help himself: he stands next to his brother, looking out. (*Beat.*) But the father doesn't get out of the car. It's five thirty. He's watching the fog creep up the inside of the windshield. It's six, he's parked in his driveway. Six thirty. He does this some nights. It's seven o'clock. (I know what he's doing, Bob. He's making a promise to himself, again and again: I promise not to start the car, not to back out on to the road, not to drive away.) Another hour passes. The keys are in the ignition. (All you have to do is turn it, is all it takes, it's all you have to do.) He touches the keys. He tastes a little puke at the back of his throat. (*Beat.*) He gets out of the car. (*Beat.*) Inside, the little one yelps, a squeal of anticipation, and they run to their bedroom. They get their pajamas on. They whisper, and the whispering makes them laugh. Their father's home. (*Beat.*) The kids come into the kitchen (they come in here) to find him sitting at the table, eating. He's got a piece of bread and a glass of water. The boys stand side by side, near the stove and they watch him. The sound of them watching presses on the back of his neck, and he wonders which one is the German shepherd, which one is the guard. He decides the older one is handcuffs and maybe the other one is more like a rotting mattress. (*Beat.*) But the boys, though, the boys are mesmerized. They watch him chew. They watch him swallow. Drink water from his glass. He's fascinating. This is how it's been, for as long as they've been alive, and still, they gape at the father eating: maybe this time he'll melt, maybe he'll turn to glass, or turn around, or choke, or maybe this time he'll speak to us. (*Beat.*) Then the father stands. The boys know their signal. They hurry off to bed. They lie under the covers thinking about tomorrow, thinking: Maybe tomorrow. (*Beat.*) The next morning, the younger one wakes up early. You wake up to pee. You come back, you stand by my bed, breathing. (*Pause.*) You say, 'Where's Daddy?'

Pause.

On an average day, he left us. That's who your father is.

Beat. **Jack** *has held the pistol since he fired it. He now offers it to* **Robert**.

I want you to take this.

Robert   I have a different idea. How about you get out of my house.

Jack   Bob?

Robert   Get out.

Jack (*a confession*)   I have two children.

Pause.

I have two children.

Robert *attacks his brother. A titanic fist fight. Fists, feet, pots and pans, bottles, tables and chairs.* **Robert** *fights in a rage. He is out to wound.* **Jack** *fights defensively, at first. He parries. A pause in the fight.*

Jack (*inviting* **Robert** *to hurt him*)   Come on, Bobby.

And then **Jack** *stops defending himself. He accepts blows. Finally,* **Jack** *is thrown to the ground, at the base of the sink.* **Robert** *faces him, winded.*

Robert   You know, if you have a bit of the black plague, Jack? You don't go around shakin' hands with the neighbors.

Jack   I'll keep that in mind.

Robert   (Don't you try to get friendly on me, Jackson.)

Jack   (I'm just sitting here.)

Robert   What, you thought you needed a coupla *heirs*? Thought you might infect a whole extra *generation*?

Robert *lifts a chair from the kitchen table above his head.* **Jack** *is below him. The coming blow would injure* **Jack**, *surely.* **Robert** *hesitates. Pause.*

Jack (*gently urging*)   It's OK, Bobby.

Robert *drops the chair, unable to administer the blow. He turns from* **Jack**, *and walks away.*

Robert   (Christ.)

Jack *reaches behind him, into a drawer. He withdraws a knife.*

Jack   Bob, pick up the gun.

Robert (*turns, sees the knife*)   (You know, if an alien landed in the kitchen, he sees you make that request?)

Jack   Pick it up.

Robert   (What's he think is going on here, Jack?)

Jack   Now, Bobby.

Robert *lifts the gun from the floor.* **Jack** *places the knife on the counter. They stand facing one another. Pause.*

Robert (*sadly*)   I just try to keep breathing. (*Beat.*) When in doubt? I just do everything I can to keep breathing air. (God.) You make it difficult, Jack. You make it hard. (*Pause.*) Can I ask you something?

Jack   Sure.

Robert (*openly*)   What do you want?

Pause.

Jack   (Bob?)

Robert   Isn't that a reasonable question?

Jack   It is.

Robert   What are you doing here?

Jack   (Hey, Bobby?)

Robert   (Yeah.)

Jack   I have two children.

Robert (*without rancour*)   You said that.

Jack   Two kids.

Robert   I heard you, Jack.

Jack   And a wife.

Pause.

I haven't heard my name. (I don't know how long it's been.) I haven't heard my name out loud.

Pause.

Robert   Why?

Jack   She thinks I'm deaf. Thinks I'm hard of hearing, but it's not my name she's calling. (We're like dogs. I didn't used to know this, but if it's not your own name? You don't *hear* it. It doesn't register.) If my back is turned? I can't tell who she's talking to.

Robert   Your *wife*, you're talking about?

Pause. **Jack** *doesn't answer.*

What's she think your *name* is?

Jack (*holding out his hand waist-high*)   The older one is this big. A boy.

Robert   You have a son.

Jack   I was out on the porch, Bobby?

Robert   How old is he?

Jack   I get off work sometimes and I stand out there.

Robert   You have a *son*, Jack?

Jack   I must've been out there a couple of *hours* or more and she sends the boy out. She got tired of yelling and she sends him out to get me. (*Beat.*) But then I don't remember it, Bobby.

Robert   You don't *remember* it?

Jack   He came out, then I was inside, that's all I know.

Robert   What happened?

Jack   When I get inside, he's crying.

Pause.

Robert   Why.

Jack   I don't know.

Robert   What'd You Do to him?

Jack   She's holding him, she says. What did you do, I say nothing, she says, What did you *do* to him, I say nothing, I see he's crying, She says, What Did You *Do* To Him.

Pause.

I got in the car this morning, I noticed something. (*Beat.*) (When I was small? He used to let me into his lap. Have me in his lap when he drove, if I begged him. He'd let you steer. You put your hands on the wheel and he'd wrap his big hands around yours. His voice was right there in your ear and his breath. Faster, Daddy. I plead with him: Faster.)

Pause.

I left them this morning, Bob.

Pause.

Up at seven, little coffee, got in the car and left. (She thought my name was Paul. It just came out. At the time, there's not a Plan. She's says, So what's your name and you go on from there.)

Beat.

I wanted a family. (*Beat.*) I just wanted a family. (*Beat.*) I started from scratch: a name, clothes, a job, all new materials. I was gonna be Sturdy, Bobby, and Safe. Come on in, it's warm, come sit by the fire. I was gonna be a Home. (*Beat.*) And I thought I built him just right, but after a while . . . I went deaf. I dried up and now he's a tomb. I'm inside here somewhere, working the levers. (*Beat.*) I try to pull the right one when the kid's crying, I try to make the thing smile . . . but the boy can see you. He knows you. Out on the porch, he sees you struggling like hell to make it smile, and he sees you fail. (*Beat.*) What must have happened out there, it happens all the time, now: I tried to smile at him and I scared him half out of his mind.

Pause.

I got in the car, this morning. (He used to wrap his big hands around mine, when I was small.) I got in the car, and I saw something, coming out of my sleeves: I saw His hands on the steering wheel.

Pause.

I left my family.

Pause.

Robert   You came here.

Jack   I drove straight here.

Robert   You want me to kill you.

Jack   I wanted to give you the opportunity.

Pause.

Robert   Oh, Jack.

Jack   I left here, you were fifteen.

Robert   Oh no, come on.

Jack   You were a kid.

Robert   I was all right.

Jack   You were a child.

Robert   You were grown *up*, Jack, you had things you had to do.

Jack   I left you.

Robert   I came out fine.

Jack (*sadly*)   Bobby, look at you. (*Beat.*) Look what happened to you.

Pause. **Jack** *crosses to* **Robert. Robert** *still holds the gun.* **Jack** *kneels before* **Robert**.

He's gone, but I'm right here. Let's put an end to it, Bobby.

Pause.

Robert You're ashamed?

Jack Please.

Robert You're ashamed?

Pause.

What's his name?

Beat.

That kid you got, your son, what's that boy's name?

Pause.

(*Simply.*) Tell you something, Jackie. I'd give my right arm to be that kid. To trade places with that kid of yours, Jack? I'd give my right arm and my left. Both my legs to be that kid. I'd give my life. (You think you let me down? You weren't brother enough? You weren't my father enough?)

Beat.

I would give the world to have you be my daddy again.

Pause.

What's his name? What's his name, Jack?

Jack . . . Peter.

Robert You tell Peter I *know* who his father is. When you talk to him? Tell him I *know* his old man.

Pause.

Jack Bobby.

Robert Go home, Jack.

Pause.

Robert You wanna do what he'd do? Die. That'd be him, probably. Go *home*. It's as unlike him as you're ever gonna be able to do: show up at your house, tell 'em Honey I'm home.

Pause.

How about a beer, Jackson.

He crosses to the refrigerator. He opens it, unhurriedly. He removes two beers, closes the refrigerator.

(Smells in there.)

He sits on the floor, by his brother. He opens **Jack***'s beer, hands it to him.* **Robert** *watches him, administering.* **Jack** *drinks.*

There you go.

Pause. **Jack** *breathes.*

(*Reassuringly.*) There it is.

Jack (*whispering*)   (I can hear my heart beating.)

Robert   (That's a good sign, Jack.)

Jack   (It's loud.)

Robert   (The way I look at it? That's a good fucking sign right there.)

Pause. He hands the gun to **Jack**.

Here. (*Beat.*) Unload it. Now, Jack. I'm sick of the fucking thing.

Jack *unloads the pistol, letting the bullets and casings fall to the floor.*

Robert   Thatta boy.

Pause.

(*Consolingly.*) All right, we're gonna be fine.

Jack   You're going to jail.

Robert   Yeah. (*Beat.*) Yeah, there is that, I guess.

Pause.

Jack   What if we left here, Bobby?

Pause.

What if we got outta here?

Robert   No. No, Jack. You go. You go home.

Jack   Come with me.

Robert   Come on. I'm gonna live fifty years in your basement? Fuck 'em. Seriously. What's that saying?

Pause.

(Doesn't exactly spring to mind, does it.)

Jack   I'm sorry, Bobby.

Robert   I'm gonna be fine.

Jack   I'm sorry.

Robert (*bravely*)   Why don't you go on now, Jack? It's OK. I don't think we wanna draw the bastard out too much.

Pause.

Jack (*still seated*)   (All right.)

Robert (*a sad little joke*)   Unless you wanna . . . take a quick shower or anything.

Pause. **Jack** *stands.*

Jack (*trying to make this true*)   I'm just going, Bob. I'm not leaving.

Robert   We'll be all right.

Jack   I'm not leaving.

Robert   You go ahead now.

Jack   We're gonna be all right, Bobby.

Pause.

Robert   Goodbye, Jack.

Jack   Goodbye.

Jack *exits*.

Pause.

Lights.

My soul is more than matched; she's overmanned; and by a madman! Insufferable sting, that sanity should ground arms on such a field! But he drilled deep down, and blasted all my reason out of me! I think I see his impious end; but feel that I must help him to it. Will I, nill I, the ineffable thing has tied me to him; tows me with a cable I have no knife to cut.

– Herman Melville